SOBRIETY IN YOUR POCKET.

DEDICATION

This work is dedicated to the most amazing person in my recovery from alcohol use disorder, my counselor in treatment. Her firm consistent support broke through my denial and saved my life. She had the skills and courage to challenge me when I was at my worst, and the love and compassion to care for me until I could care for myself.

To my sponsor who showed me by her example how to keep going and find long term freedom from alcohol by showing me a new way of living was possible, and giving me hope.

And to my beloved brother, who sadly lost his struggle with alcohol and life. Finally, to anyone suffering from the no fault illness of Aud. You can recover!

Sobriety in Your Pocket

Why quit alcohol?

Most of us can think of areas of our lives which could be improved, if we were able to make changes to our physical or emotional condition. It may be something in our lives that we no longer want to experience, such as lack of confidence, jealously or grief. Or it maybe some really awful events from our past that keep coming back to haunt us, like alcohol use disorder, (Aud).

Help isn't sometime in your future. It's now. If alcohol is holding you back from being the person you want to be, and you want to find a more manageable, happier way of life without it, you can.

Sobriety in your Pocket aims to inspire and support you when you decide to quit alcohol and open your mind to start on your way to finding a better life.

To do this you will need to be completely honest with yourself. Ask yourself, what is the problem? Is your life out of control because you can't stop drinking alcohol when you want to? What excuses or lies do use to explain your drinking and behavior to others?

You may need professional help to quit alcohol safely, so see your GP. If you do decide you do have Aud then accept the illness alcohol use disorder at gut level. Because being a sufferer of Aud is like being pregnant, you either are, or you aren't. You can't be a little bit. The great thing is you don't have to continue to suffer alone.

And here's the good news. If you are desperate enough to own your illness and all its negative consequences, you can begin to manage the disorder and recover by joining a local Aud support group and asking some one to sponsor you in to recovery.

Start by looking honestly at your history of alcohol use. Own your truth and accept you are powerless over alcohol by recognizing times you couldn't stop drinking after starting. List the times alcohol has made your life unmanageable.

The reason you have been unable to control your alcohol use even though it made your life unmanageable is because you have an illness called alcohol use disorder, or Aud.

When you can accept your illness like any other, and all its' consequences, you are ready to quit alcohol if you honestly want to. There is no cure. But there is a way of managing your condition on a daily basis to give you respite from Aud's progressive fatal symptoms if you are able to be honest, open your mind to learning and willing to change your old ways.

If you are not convinced by your own experiences to stop using alcohol, then carry on drinking until you are ready to quit and get help. Meanwhile, ask yourself how much do you have to lose to become ready to quit alcohol? How much has alcohol already cost you, in addition to the money you paid for it, eg arguments, accidents, loss of your friends, family, job, driving license. What are the benefits to you continuing to drink alcohol and harming yourself and others? How does denying the truth that you are powerless over alcohol and your life is unmanageable, help you?

Nearly 3 million people die each year from the affects of alcohol, because of their deep rooted resistance to being honest with themselves and admitting that they are powerless to quit drinking.

Illnesses that can be caused by Aud include pancreatitis, fatty liver disease, diabetes, heart disease, strokes, damage to the nervous system, mental illness, dementia, alzheimers, vascular problems, gout and gastro intestinal bleeding amongst others.

Cancers commonly associated with Aud include mouth, throat, stomach, breast, and pancreatic cancers. Pregnant women can put the fetus at risk of physical and developmental problems from Fetal Alcohol Syndrome.

A major benefit of going to an Aud support group is that others in recovery can help you to see your illness honestly when you can't see it for yourself or be rational. And you'll no longer be alone trying to manage your illness.

Breaking through your denial and accepting the illness is the first step in recovery. It's difficult, because denial is the shock absorber of the soul. It keeps you stuck, protecting you from seeing the futility and hopelessness of your illness so that it doesn't completely over whelm you.

Denial is also a symptom of the underlying mental illness caused by Aud, making you angry and dishonest, lying and excusing of your alcohol use, when challenged about your thinking or behavior. It often ends in crisis.

Science shows that people with Aud are the victims of a mental obsession to drink alcohol that they can't manage to over come it on their own. In addition they have a physical allergy to alcohol that makes them crave more, whenever they drink any at all. Chemically compelling them to continue drinking alcohol, without help to quit, they will eventually die.

As you begin to learn more about your self, you'll feel less threatened by others opinions, values and beliefs, and more accepting of others ideas.

Look back at your life history to see when your life became unmanageable because of your drinking alcohol. Recognize how ill you are and how necessary it is for you to quit alcohol and commit to opening your mind to learning how to change and recover.

If you have reached a point when you can't live with alcohol and you can't live without it, you will need help, to quit alcohol completely or the mental obsession to use alcohol will start you drinking again.

You need to be honest with your self, friends and family, stop covering up your deceitful behavior, lies, cheating, exaggeration about the mistakes you made while drinking alcohol.

Joining a local Aud support group, doing what others in recovery suggest and accepting your truth, are vital for helping you break through your denial. To stand any chance of finding recovery and gain the knowledge you need to change your attitude to alcohol you need to stop being self-centered and accept you can't drink safely gain.

But be warned. Quitting alcohol and working to establish your recovery can sometimes feel like a game of 'Whack- a-Mole'. As you deal with one addiction, another may appear, demanding your attention by causing you harm, eg over eating.

Alcohol is a fiendish deadly habit. Now that you know your mental obsession compels you to use alcohol you'll need to do whatever it takes not to drink if you want to stay manageable. This obsession is the part of Aud illness that you may experience in the future making it hard for you to continue to stay stopped.

But by regularly attending Aud meetings and sharing with recovering others, you can begin to like yourself again and easily learn how to manage the lies your head tells you, to start to enjoy recovery.

Quitting alcohol offers you a powerful way of finding out who you really are. Exploring what you think, feel, know, understand and remember about your journey so far, can help you can decide which areas of your life to change for a better future ,eg lying, blaming, selfishness, controlling and self-pitying.

By honestly becoming ready to change, you can let go of your obsessive thinking and self-pity about the changes you face. You can ask for the help you need to recover, and have faith in your inner resources to guide you in your daily business. All you need is an open mind and the willingness to follow your inner power, rather than your head. Reckless, behavior is irresponsible. Sober you can accept responsibility for your self, your thoughts, actions behaviors and feelings and begin to feel better about your self.

You know from your own history of using alcohol that your self will is weak and ineffectual against your obsession to drink. But if you are desperate for relief and prepared to do whatever it takes to find recovery, then you will be ready to let go of your thinking and let your inner power and others in your Aud group guide you.

Relieved of your obsession to drink alcohol you will be able to change your thinking and in time turn your life around. Within days you will feel better, look better and enjoy having more energy and stop hurting yourself and others. In a month your Jekyll and Hyde personality will be more balanced making life more manageable.

Identifying your unhelpful thoughts and ideas will help you to accept your reality and continue to break through any lingering denial you may have had of your problem. This is important for you when making the decision to change. But it does take time to learn about your self and become willing to change your thinking and behavior so you won't want to use alcohol again.

Because your drinking is reactionary, you use alcohol to medicate life's pain you'll soon see how you are the creator of all your problems. The marvelous thing is that because you do the drinking, you can decide to take responsibility for your behavior and stop drinking.

It's quite simple to see your part in your illness and understand your actions and reactions when they are written down. Nothing is ever solved by wishing on a star. Give up magical thinking and accept responsibility for your self by asking some one from your Aud group to sponsor you in to recovery.

The choice is now yours. Learn how to take care of yourself and how to ask for help; let go of your fear and mistrust, and accept your need to change your life and recover from Aud. For the time and effort it takes to learn how to change your thinking and behavior and quit alcohol for good, it really is worth deciding to try it. After three days without alcohol the biochemical craving for more will be gone. But biological healing from Aud takes longer.

Let go of worry for the future and decide to keep going and going until you feel better, because you will. I guarantee if do what is suggested, change your thinking, work hard and develop your faith in the power already inside you, rather than follow your head you can not fail to find rewarding recovery from any addiction. You can eliminate alcohol or anything else unwanted in your life, for good.

No matter who you are, or where you are in your journey of life, tragedy can happen because that is life on life's terms. These things, and other events, like having to let go of alcohol, just happen. But after your grief and anger you can experience the freedom acceptance of the situation eventually brings.

Stave off any cravings by eating or drinking sugary things, – **you can** diet later.

After a couple weeks not using alcohol you can expect your appetite to return and to be able to sleep better. You'll start to feel better and look better. People will notice improvement in your dry hair and blotchy face and flaky skin. You'll begin to look younger and enjoy having more energy, too. You'll be able to share your experiences with others and trust your self more.

Science shows it takes at least six weeks to get rid of an unwanted habit. What's more, healing from Aud closely resembles healing from a stroke. It demands deliberate, determined ongoing effort to do the mind work needed to deal with the obsessive thinking and achieve neurological changes vital to recovery.

Because the principles of recovery from Aud are the same as the universal principles for living, you'll need to open your mind to a new way of thinking and behaving to continue in your recovery. Your sponsor can help you to find freedom from Aud. The same principles can free you from any other addiction you want to be free from.

Understanding your alcohol disorder and joining an Aud group and getting a sponsor, are essential to you getting well. Doing these few simple things offers you the support, tools and techniques you need to successfully overcome your illness. Like following the recipe for making a cake, you will be given all the ingredients necessary for you to achieve a better way of living a happy and purposeful life. If you don't follow the recipe you won't get the cake you want.

So the quality of your recovery depends on the work you do and effort you make. Let go of self-pity and follow the suggestions of those in recovery. In time and with practice you will change.

By exploring your journey so far and reconnecting with your real self, you will be able to make better choices in your future without needing relief from alcohol.

Unlike medicine, anyone can use the suggestions in this guide to connect and learn more about themselves if they want to change their situation.

Connection is all about how we feel about ourselves and other people. Awareness of self is vital for anyone to accept their need to change their feelings and reconnect with themselves, their friends and family.

Take a good hard honest look at your alcohol use. Willingness to act on the decision to change and stop using alcohol is dependent on how you see yourself.

We all connect to someone, though not always positively. The saying, 'birds of a feather flock together,' is often true enough, just like the saying 'misery loves company,' probably because these people tend to attract others on the same wave length, sharing a similar view of the world and sense of purpose, often in the pub.

Open your mind to letting go of negative influences eg stay out of wet places or you'll take a drink, because if you go to the hairdressers often enough, you're sure to get a hair cut.

How do you stay well? You get honest; you open your mind to learning from others who have recovery and you become willing to change your life around. Take responsibility for your actions and own your drinking habits and the consequences eg lying, being offensive, out of control, selfish, abusive.

Practice checking your thinking. Be aware of your negative feelings. Name them and do something different until they pass eg ring someone, take some exercise, sing, dance go for a run or take yourself off to bed to stay safe and sleep it off.

As you begin to recognize and develop positive characteristics and take more responsibility for your behavior, you'll start to feel more self worth.

Changing your thoughts before they become obsessive and take you over is vital to you managing your new life in recovery and maintaining your sobriety.

You may still be having bad feelings and mood swings. But it's only acting on them that make things bad. In time they'll pass. If you feel frustrated and alone, focus on connecting with yourself and other Aud sufferers. No body died because of what they were feeling. They died because of what they did with those feelings.

Keep going to meetings especially when you don't want to. Share your feelings. Listen to others experiences. Know that you are not alone with your struggles. Recommit daily to doing what ever it takes to get to bed that night without using alcohol and call yourself a winner, because that is what you'll be.

Don't sit with yourself while you go through a period of struggling. There's bound to be a period of adjustment living without alcohol. Talk to your sponsor or other Aud friends. You'll understand others more easily and feel empathy for them.

When you struggle, remind yourself exactly what it is you'll be missing by not using alcohol. Then honestly list the benefits to you of not using alcohol and choose what's best for you. The support of others can strengthen your determination to change and succeed as you work with a sponsor to find recovery.

Aud is the most expensive group you'll ever join! So get stuck in and learn from the others in the 'I can do club' how to stay well long term. I promise if they can quit alcohol then you can, too. And remember the real problem is alcohol, not you. All you have to do is decide to quit alcohol, stay sober and manage your day in recovery.

Imagine how freeing it will be when you turn all your negative feelings around and take back control of your life. You can start that change right now, by realizing the impact your feelings have on you, and making the decision to stop using alcohol. Stick with the winners not the whiners, and I guarantee if you stay sober you will find a much better and happier way of living. It's not about your background. It's about you being honest and making the effort you need to gct well.

If you wanted to learn to drive, you'd go to driving lessons. If you want to learn how to stay sober you need to go to Aud meetings and take lessons in how to stay sober lessons. It's simple. If you don't take the first drink, you can't get drunk.

The past has gone, except in your mind, so dwelling on your mistakes and hurts stops you from being in the present. As German writer Eckart Tolle said, 'if you're focusing on your past or on your future when you arrive, you're not all there.'

If your struggling put a spoon of cinnamon in you breakfast drink to help regulate your blood sugars and reduce the mental somersaults. What you think certainly can have big impact on your sense of well- being. Picture a good outcome or end result to a problem you have, in your mind and trust your inner power that things will work out okay. Focus on the result and get closer to your goal. It may not always be what you want. But almost certainly it will turn out to be what you need.

List all the times in your day you're going to find hard while quitting alcohol. And then match each time with a sugary drink fix. When that difficult time arrives in your day, try to wait 20 minutes before having your sugary fix and note how the craving shifts as your 'I can do this' thinking develops

A helpful acronyms is HALT; meaning hunger, anger, loneliness and tiredness. Any of these conditions that goes unmet, can quickly undermine your resolve not to drink. Check how you feel regularly and be alerted to the need for change to maintain your well being. You may need to talk, or eat something or rest.

If all else fails, go back to basics and check your feelings out. It's a great way to improve looking after your self. Like approaching red traffic lights we need to stop and check how we feel. Amber means get ready to act to change any negative feeling. And green gives the okay to move forward safely.

Following the same principles of making your thinking positive every day, you can soon replace old unhelpful habits with good more helpful ones. In time this is how you'll change, always remembering that the goal is progress and not perfection.

Treat yourself gently, but keep going to Aud meetings to learn more about recovery. Ask for any help you need to change your thinking and embrace changing your behavior in the future. Let go of your need to control and stop fighting against giving up alcohol. What are you honestly being deprived of? Your way never worked.

The fact is recovery from Aud begins as soon as you stop using alcohol. But if you have been on the path to addiction for some time you may need more help. You may have lost touch with your values and beliefs and may have problems coming to terms with your behavior or other consequences of using alcohol eg self limiting beliefs, guilt for wrong doing or shame that you are simply a no good human being.

Get a sponsor to guide you towards getting rid of this self harming image of yourself. No one is worthless or all bad. Naturally it will take time to get used to doing something different. If your life has felt like going from crisis to crisis because of you using alcohol eg financial, family and health problems, losing friends, your job, not managing your life.

You will have to practice changing old ways of thinking and feeling and behaving for several weeks to change the habits you've engaged in for your life time.

Imagine yourself sober in a hot air balloon, floating up over your self at a summer picnic. How amazing it could be seeing you and people you know and love sitting about in the sunshine eating and drinking soft drinks and chatting together happily.

Maybe your shame has kept you unknowingly self-sabotaging and returning to alcohol because you don't believe you deserve to succeed. But now you can believe it if you keep going and follow the suggestions in this guide, I guarantee you'll succeed.

Facing the consequences of a chaotic life is never easy. But, you can have hope, because as you work on changing your thinking and feeling and start to change on the inside, everything outside will start to change, too.

Make a daily gratitude list. This is a really powerful recovery tool because experience shows a truly grateful alcoholic doesn't want to drink alcohol.

What are you waiting for? Seize the moment and make your promise to yourself today. Decide to start your first day in recovery now, not when.

So what is Aud? Aud is a 'no fault' illness that results in a physical craving for more alcohol despite negative consequences, because of a mental obsession to drink.

The facts show that addiction of any kind changes the brains neuro-pathways, damaging the frontal lobes that are responsible for judgment, perception and common sense. These biological changes are clearly nothing to do with a lack of will power or poor moral judgment. Alcohol is the problem, and Aud is an illness, recognized since 1957 by the World Health Organization.

While the need for alcohol is always psychological, it can be physical, too. Withdrawing suddenly can be unsafe. For this reason, you ought to consult your GP. As the individual's tolerance grows they drink more alcohol to get the 'effect' they need to manage feelings they can't openly express. Aud is therefore an emotional as well as a mental illness. Few sufferers are able to stop using alcohol without help.

No body asks to have their dignity taken away from them. Nobody asks to feel lonely or confused. The fact is people with Aud don't produce enough enzymes to break down and process alcohol fully, like other drinkers do.

People with Aud will never be able to drink safely. The mental obsession to use alcohol for instant gratification to change how they feel is a real PIG of a problem, leaving them powerless over alcohol. The only relief is to find a new power to drive the pig away. Your body can't tolerate alcohol and your mind won't let you leave it alone.

List three times you told yourself you could drink alcohol safely even though your experience shows you can't control how much you drink any more than King Knut could hold back the sea. How is your behavior different to others who drink?

To do this successfully means you must let go of your controlling behaviors and accept your way doesn't work. Swallow your pride and open your mind to the idea of relying on a different power to your own self will to guide you in life.

Finding a new power to guide you is essential to finding recovery. Are you willing to believe in something more powerful than your self? eg what ever it is that makes the grass grow- because it isn't you.

The lie that you'll be able to use alcohol like other people is the root of your powerlessness and insanity. This symptom of Aud is the mental obsession you suffer from. The problem is it comes to mind while you're not drinking alcohol.

Certain things can trigger you to think of using alcohol, eg people, places, music, food, stress. List the things that trigger you and be ready to act differently.

In your past you hung on to this insane thought or 'mental twist' until it grew into an obsession, replacing any other ideas you had, making it impossible for you to stop drinking of your own free will. Now you can choose to act instead of react, eg don't think don't drink ring somebody and talk.

This stinking thinking is probably the most difficult part of recovering from Aud because you will always have that mental obsession. While the sensation is elusive and you know drinking is harmful, you can easily lose sight of reality, and start drinking again if you don't do the mind work needed to change your thinking.

So the real problem is with the way you think. It's faulty, telling you it is okay to drink, even though your body ensures that you can not drink, safely. No matter what you do, your will power is not enough to handle the problem.

However, if you are willing to believe and have faith in your higher power, you can turn your faulty thinking over, and do something different until it has passed, without needing to drink.

Everyone has a sense of some sort of higher power inside them. Belief in this inner higher power is essential to finding sanity and long term recovery. If you are convinced by your alcohol history that you are powerless over alcohol and it is making your life unmanageable then you must find a higher power you can trust.

Begin by deciding what you think you believe in. Then, make with the action needed to try out your belief, eg if you take your shoes to the cobblers to be fixed, the cobbler will fix them. When you get your shoes back you can see if your belief was correct. If you find the cobbler has done a good job, you'll use him again because now you can trust and have faith in him to do a good job the same next time you ask him.

List all the times something has been looking after you.

Remember, you're not mad, or bad, or sad; you have a no fault illness. Like diabetes, Aud needs to be managed on a daily basis so you can recover and not die.

That's not to say recovery is easy, but others in your Aud group are proof that it is doable. And if they can do it, then so can you.

Knowing what you now know, that there is a solution to your addiction, you no longer have any honest excuse to carry on drinking your self to death. Let yourself enjoy the good things in your life.

The pathology shows Aud is a chronic, progressive and fatal illness if left untreated. What's more, it usually develops slowly and subtly. The sufferer seldom notices the harmful changes Aud causes them or their family, until they are quite ill. Left unchecked Aud is relentless, quickly becoming uncontrollable and fatal.

In the later stages of Aud the sufferer's body starts to give up and physical difficulties become more severe ending with insanity or death, due to one thing or another eg liver, lung, heart or pancreas failure, suicide accident or violence.

The Physical Problem of Aud was first explained by American doctor of neurology called Silkworth as being an allergy to alcohol, means you can't ever drink safely.

The Neuro - Science behind the illness confirms the nature of Aud, showing the brain chemistry of sufferers is different to that of other people. Biochemical processes show alcohol changes the drinker's neuro pathways which create a bio chemical craving for more alcohol, regardless of its harmful consequences.

This means the Aud sufferer loses all choice over alcohol meaning they are powerless to control their drinking. They continue to drink alcohol because they have to, not because they choose to. Without help to quit alcohol they will carry on drinking until they are dead.

But to make any changes, you need to be willing. If you are honest and look at your history with alcohol, you'll be able to identify times when your drinking has been out of control and made your life unmanageable. Then you can decide if you have Aud and are ready to change.

If you continue to drink alcohol in spite of all the bad things that have happened to you and don't change your thinking, your life will spiral out of control. If you quit using alcohol but don't do the mind changing work needed for recovery, you will be a dry drunk- and as miserable as a wood pecker without a beak. Feeling deprived dissatisfied and discontent you'll most probably end up using alcohol again.

So what is the solution? Do what ever it takes just for today not to drink alcohol. Commit to attending your local Aud group asking for the help you need to change your behavior to learn how to quit alcohol and practice living in sobriety, one day at a time. You may not want to, but you need to, because you can't stay sober alone.

To help you accept your truth make a list of times you started drinking again when you really didn't want to, and times when you wanted to stop drinking but really couldn't put alcohol down when you wanted to. Look at your examples and consider what you have lost because of your drinking, eg friends, family jobs self respect.

Describe how your behavior shows you are powerless over alcohol and out of control of your drinking? eg hiding how much you drink from others, lying and making excuses for continuing to use alcohol, getting into situations where your use of alcohol and behavior is different from other people.

If you have decided you can't drink safely because you are powerless over alcohol and it makes your life unmanageable, then the obvious answer is to quit using it, and deal with your feelings in a more manageable and better way for yourself. You must find a different coping mechanism; a different power to run your life, and let go of your self–will, your faulty thinking and need to control.

Just for today, commit to doing whatever it takes not to drink alcohol. The great thing about your story is that you never have to feel helpless and desperate, or alone again. Once you understand the real nature of your condition and quit alcohol you can step in to the solution by swallowing your pride and opening your mind to the idea of finding a different power to run your life and guide you. And the most marvelous thing is you already have that power you need to change, inside you.

Relying on your inner power rather than your old thinking, is essential to you being able to find recovery, because your best thinking won't keep you sober.

You are what you think so how you behave depends on your thoughts and how you think determines your life. If your thinking is okay, good okay actions are likely to follow, so your life has more chance of being okay, too.

Left on your own resources, you're going to do the same things you've always done, feel guilt-ridden and ashamed and be filled with unhappiness so that you use alcohol again to change how you feel. But does alcohol really make you feel better?

Right or wrong, real or imagined, your beliefs determine how you see things, your attitude and your behavior. Practice listening to your inner voice or higher power. By tuning into the extended and incredible power of the universe, you'll move from your old self-reliance, to a reliance on spiritual direction. Becoming more connected to your self and others will boost your sense of belonging.

Learning how to be balanced and flexible will help you to keep your edge and follow the infinite wisdom of your higher Power.

Take time to be still and think. Get away on your own and listen to your inner voice or higher power. New goals will keep you moving forward. Goals give us a purpose. Whatever yours is, define it clearly, then go to work on achieving it.

Start by being quiet and listening to yourself. When the answer comes it will be so obvious and clear and simple you can't miss it. You'll feel energized and excited. Everything you need to change your life is within your own reach. So make success a habit and confidently follow your desires to improve your self by doing more worth while things.

Of course, you'll need to be disciplined, because you can't recover on your own. You need the help of your higher power to follow up your goals with right actions, to live a meaningful life and achieve what you want. With continued practice you'll be just as capable of endurance as anyone else in recovery.

As you grow in recovery and become more aware of your character defects you get more familiar with dealing with everyday life as it unfolds. You recognize your wrong doings more quickly and more readily take the action to right them, respond to your wrong doing, and the ways you fall short of how you want to be.

Routine work on your self and your behavior affects others as well as going to meetings helps keep up the momentum of recovery. This is important in helping you to change from learning how to stay away from alcohol, to feeling comfortable choosing to live in sobriety.

The Neuro Science shows the most incredible fact underlying recovery from Aud is that we know, through measurable biochemical process, anyone can recover from alcohol or any other addiction. By changing your thinking you can change the neuro –pathways of the brain and messages they carry so the old neuro pathways become obsolete, like an unused forest pathway quickly becomes overgrown and impassable

So if you want to stop drinking alcohol and be happy, you need to change your thinking and personality. Continuing to run your life on self-will can hardly be successful. Somewhere deep inside yourself you've always known right from wrong. But your own thinking has always taken over. The problem is if you suffer with Aud, your best thinking can't stop you drinking because of your mental obsession for alcohol.

Take time to talk to your higher power, about every aspect of your life. You'll intuitively learn to recognize right from wrong and know what to do. Ask for help to know what is best for you to do. You are stronger than you think. You can recover.

Humble your self and open your heart to hear your higher power's messages coming back. Let go of your self will and desire to control everything and become willing to learn and change. As you learn to trust in your higher power your negative feelings will pass and doing the right thing will come more naturally to you.

The lie ('you'll be able to use alcohol like other people') is the root of your insanity. It's a symptom of Aud that comes to mind while you're not drinking alcohol.

In your past this insane thought or 'mental twist' would grow into an obsession caused by your disorder, replacing any other ideas you have, making it impossible for you to stop drinking of your own free will.

This is the most difficult part of alcohol misuse. However, the sensation is so elusive, that while you know drinking is harmful, you lose sight of reality, and normalize abnormal behavior.

You know the real problem is with the way you think. It's faulty, telling you it is okay to drink, even though your body is allergic to alcohol so you can not drink, safely. No matter what you do, your will power is not enough to handle the problem.

However, if you are willing to believe and have faith in your higher power, you can turn your faulty thinking over, and do something different until it has passed, without needing to drink.

Everyone has a sense of some sort of higher power inside them. Belief in this inner resource is essential to finding sanity and long term recovery. If you are convinced by your alcohol history that you are powerless and your life is unmanageable then you must find your higher power and start trusting in it.

Begin by deciding what you think you believe in. Then, take the action needed to try out what you believe, eg taking your shoes to the cobblers to be fixed, to see if your belief was correct. If you find they do a good job, the next time you'll go back to them because you can trust and have faith in them, based on your past experience.

List all the times something has been looking after you. Ask yourself: is it odd or is it God?

The world is a dynamic and fantastic place full of opportunities. Of course it takes time and practice to develop the habit of handing your will over to your higher power. But in time it will become a natural habit. You will be more mindful and aware of how you feel and what is going on around you. With discipline and determination, you can let go of self will and let your higher power guide you.

At gut level you do know right from wrong, so the choice to change is really up to you. Practice letting go of your unhelpful thinking and do what you feel is right. Follow your higher power, not your head. Be honest, because by now you know if you suffer from Aud, your best thinking won't keep you sober.

The way you think has a big impact on your sense of well- being.

Picture a good outcome or end result to a problem you have, in your mind and trust your higher power that things will work out okay. Focus on the result and get closer to your goal. It may not always be what you want. But almost certainly it will turn out to be what you need.

By following the same principles every day you can soon replace old unhelpful habits with good more helpful ones. This is how you really can change, always remembering that the goal is progress and not perfection.

It will take time to get used to doing something different. But if your life has felt like going from crisis to crisis because of using alcohol eg financial, family and health problems, losing friends, your job, not managing your life, you can change.

Perhaps you can't imagine your life without alcohol; how amazing it can be. Maybe you have been unknowingly self-sabotaging because you don't believe you deserve to succeed. But now you can believe if you keep going to Aud meetings and follow the suggestions in this guide, you are guaranteed to succeed, and get well.

Stinking thinking; believing you can control your drinking. Letting go of the need to control everything and follow your higher power takes practice. Like stepping into the boxing ring with a world heavy weight champion like Mohamed Ali, the sooner you surrender any stinking thinking to your higher power, the sooner you will be saved from acting on your self-will and harming yourself and others. The longer you fight to get control, the more beaten and broken you'll be.

When the Emperor Hadrian realized he would lose the war he was fighting against the Parthian Empire, he withdrew his army and changed his strategy.

The world is a dynamic place and a self-willed person is extremely self- centered and difficult to be around. They always filled with fear and causing harm by trying to control. Selfishly trying to fulfill your needs by controlling others is at the heart of all your problems. So it's good for everyone that you can change this.

Practice letting go of self will and trusting in your higher power that everything will be okay as the day unfolds before you. Develop your faith in something other than your self and stop trying to fix everything to suit you. Be honest, your way never worked and it never will with you in control.

But, be gentle with yourself. Remember you have a no fault illness and need to forgive yourself. There's no need to judge yourself harshly, replaying in your mind all your mistakes and failures. Harboring guilt harms you and others, giving you a reason to drink alcohol again.

Let past events stay in your past, and focus on being positive, just for today. List the moments of love and kindness, generosity and success you've had in your past, and know that you are worthwhile. Ask yourself what you did well today and what you could do differently tomorrow. Thank your higher power for your sobriety. Letting go means looking back without regret and moving on in a better way.

Giving up your harmful attitude and behavior means stopping judging others.

William Shakespeare wrote 'there is nothing either good or bad, but thinking makes it so.' eg when you judge the weather as bad you are bound to respond with upset or anger. But when you accept the things you can't control, you are free to think more clearly about what you need to do to manage your day.

Managing your feelings without medicating with alcohol is a bit like managing a football team. If the players are no good at playing together and you feel abject despair at their performance, you need to get a new manager and team strategy.

Getting a new manager to guide the players is like you getting a new power to guide you instead of relying on alcohol. In time you learn how to play a better game and make better decisions for yourself and start winning at life.

The more willing you are to depend on your higher power the more settled and happy you'll be, accepting life on life's terms and dealing with it as it unfolds.

Blessed with the gift of desperation to change, you can leave your heavy goods wagon full of self will behind, and let your higher power run the show. In time, you will see whose will is at work, and whose will works! Be grateful to be sober.

All the noise in your head will stop when you stop controlling and let your higher power guide you. Turning things over to your higher power to manage will be incredibly freeing and healing for you. Show your gratitude by helping others.

Just like you might take your broken down car to the garage because you believe they can repair it, all you need to do to make a start at developing faith in your higher power is to act on your belief and see what the outcome is.

Admitting you have Aud is difficult. You may feel so bad about your past use of alcohol that you deny things are as bad as they or blame others. This only fills you guilt, anger and fear of being exposed.

If you have decided you do have Aud, and you're honestly willing to change then ask your higher power for help, and believe that you can get well. But recovery doesn't happen by magical thinking, or wishing on a star. You have to take the actions suggested and practice them to change your old habits and benefit from trusting in a higher power. And let's face it, how successful have you been running your own life?

Start the new day with a new determination. Thank your higher power for waking you up sober and ask to do his will, not your own during the day. Planning what you intend to do is a helpful tool. It keeps you on track so that your self-will doesn't take over leading you to behave in self-defeating ways. Keep a journal of how you think and feel throughout your day.

Journaling is really helpful to you seeing your own patterns of self destructive behavior and overcoming your resistance to changing the things you can.

Set your self an achievable goal to give you a sense of worth eg to get through the day with out drinking alcohol; I'll tidy the cupboards; I'll cut the lawn.

It's not rocket science. But if you want to feel good, you need to do good things. Having a daily goal is the magic instrument that moves you forward in life to achieving good things. Finding your higher power is absolutely vital to staying well.

You may be no more willing to believe in a higher power than you are to believe in the tooth fairy. Make a list of all the times your higher power helped you with your difficulties eg you haven't killed yourself by drink driving or fallen asleep intoxicated and burnt the house down.

Look at the unpleasant truths on your list and your harmful behaviors when you used alcohol and took control. Look at how your behavior conflicts with your values and how you are the cause of all your problems because you were controlling.

Notice when you point your finger and blame someone else, it leaves three fingers pointing back at yourself. Be honest and take responsibility for yourself.

List the troubles you have experienced in your past due to you using alcohol.

Hanging on to grudges you have against others may make you feel safe. Your anger at them will make you feel powerful and in control and less vulnerable to attack. But grudges keep you unhappy, stuck in the misery of either defending yourself or attacking others.

Let go of your controlling thoughts and behaviors and decide to forgive yourself and others to free yourself of negative feelings. That way you can see that a snake is a snake, but move away before it bites you.

Forgiveness means forgoing, or giving up your grudges allows you to go forward and open your mind and heart to experiencing new ways of seeing and connecting with others and the world. Make a list of others you could forgive and practice finding freedom by giving up your grudges against them.

Forgiveness doesn't mean you have to put up with others bad behavior towards you. It means accepting them for just what they are eg if a bully is a bully, recognize them as being a bully and move away before they hurt you. You can not change anyone. You don't have to agree with them, just recognize them for what they are eg abusive. You can't change them, only yourself. So let them go and focus on your own well-being.

Practice being grateful for your life every day, by listing what it is you are grateful for. It's a fantastic way to boost your happiness. Stand in front of the mirror and quickly grin at yourself several times. You'll soon start laughing at your self and feeling more grateful for life. This tool always works if you work it, and won't if you don't. What's important is to know you can change your negative feelings anytime you want. And when you feel grateful, you will not want to drink alcohol.

The quality of your life comes from you developing a healthy self-image as you learn to trust more in your higher power, and change your personality defects. Your personality is naturally shaped by your basic instincts which drive your behavior. You were born with three basic instincts of life necessary for your survival, self-preservation, reproduction and socialization, wanting to belong or be accepted.

Running your life on self-will to get your instincts met, has usually set you at odds with others, causing you and them, harm, eg being resentful because of misjudging others; being fearful because of not believing others; wrong doing causing you shame and remorse.

You have to give up your harmful control. It doesn't work. Throw away your old ideas and make room for new ones to come in. Go to Aud meetings and learn what others do to manage how they feel without using alcohol.

Free yourself from the need to control by trusting in your higher power to provide what you need. When you do, all sorts of amazing things will happen eg you will feel a new power inside you, freeing you from fear; you will enjoy peace of mind and realize you can face life, and whatever it brings without needing alcohol.

Trust that all will be okay and take a break before you are broken. Relax with a cup of sugary tea. Let your higher power care for you, guide you and direct your life, how you behave and what you think.

Take stock of all personality traits. Be honest and look at things as they really are. Then do a thorough moral inventory of yourself to identify the major defects you want to be rid off. This is where you see what you need to change in you, eg selfishness, fear, dishonesty.

Usually resentment or grudges and hard done by feelings cause Aud sufferers the most upset. These take all your time and energy, focusing the person you think harmed you and ignoring you higher Power. You obsessively replay events in your mind, filling with anger and self pity, and are dreadful to be around. Don't let others live in your head rent free. Turn them out to your higher power to deal with for you.

To be rid of the stubborn resentments you hold against others, look at yourself; Draw four columns across a page of paper. In the first column write down all the people, places and things eg doctor's surgeries, courts, police-stations, sod's law, that ever caused you to feel angry or upset in your life. This is quite a task, but thoroughness is the key.

When you have listed all the people, places and things that had upset you, write down the cause of your grudge or upset in the second column against each person place or thing.

Then in the third column I wrote down what part of you was upset by the person place or thing eg your self esteem, pride, relationships, material security, emotional security, acceptable sexual relationships or ambition.

Finally, honestly look at your part in each of your resentments; what did you do to cause the situation or make it worse, eg get drunk. Include where you had been selfish, inconsiderate, fearful or dishonest.

Honestly review your list of resentments with someone in recovery. Identify your part in each eg where you dishonest and selfish. Take responsibility for your own behavior. Own your part in things and let go of your unreasonable and dishonest behavior and thinking towards others by accepting nearly all your problems were caused by you drinking alcohol, not caring and behaving badly towards others.

Do a similar inventory of your fears, looking at your part in them and letting them go. Complete your inventory by listing any other problems or harms you caused, and why eg threatening a friend when they pour your drink away or refuse to lend you money to buy alcohol.

All this work on your inventory will show you how selfish and dishonest about your life and relationships you really are because of drinking alcohol. If you search honestly you'll find selfishness is at the heart of all your problems. Look at which of your life issues appear the most in your lists. It will probably be clear that the ones causing you the most hurt and upset were your self-esteem and personal relationships, because you were using alcohol and trying to control the consequences in your life.

Seeing your truth can be very upsetting for you. However, denial is the shock absorber of the soul. By checking how you feeling today and looking at your part in your problems, you can change how you feel and manage to live your life much more positively without needing alcohol. And if I can do it then so can you.

Start by trying to identify what it is you are feeling and name it eg afraid, sad, envious hurt exhausted. Then ask for the willingness to believe the feeling will pass. Own your feelings eg I'm anxious, I'm bored, I'm curious. Hand them over to your higher power, waiting quietly and patiently until the feeling passes. And it will pass.

But negative feelings will always pass a lot quicker if you talk to someone from you support group who understands your illness, or do something different to change your thinking eg make yourself laugh and feel grateful by quickly leering at your self in the mirror. It never fails because laughter is the best medicine for changing the way you feel, and it's free!

Accept your feelings are part of you, and chose how you respond to them. It helps to share how you feel rather than deny or try to control circumstances, because a problem shared is a problem halved, releasing the pressure built up inside you. And believe this; your worst day sober will never be as bad as your best day drinking.

Today we know from neuro science that feelings themselves can also be addictive: not only pleasurable feelings the adrenaline junkies chase bunging jumping and wave hopping, but emotions like anger, loneliness and grief.

Keep working on your new behaviors. It's so easy to slip into old behaviors eg when you shout at someone who has done something wrong you energize your own brain with neuro-chemicals. These chemicals are part of the brain's stress response system and connect to the brain's reward centers, so you feel good when you get angry or resentful.

Recovery is, among other positive things, a process of making sense of your life. The fact that these chemicals and feelings can be addictive, explains why some people hang on to old feelings, becoming addicted to them eg worry, misery, grandiosity.

How true it is, that worrying has never solved any problem. Like feeling guilty about things you did while drinking alcohol, it's a waste of time, filling you with negative thoughts that keep you stuck in your past.

What ever the wrong doing you did using alcohol that you feel guilty about, it's done. It's in your past. You've punished yourself enough for your old behaviors. It's time to let go and change for good. It's very simple to know the difference between right and wrong.

Turn your character defects around and practice behaving in the opposite way, eg be pleasant instead of grumpy, calm instead of angry, caring instead of uncaring and considerate instead of inconsiderate. You'll feel better about yourself, and attract similar people. Every area of your life will improve.

Because your illness left you vulnerable, you've probably experienced extreme hurt in your life, eg from broken relationships. Pain resulting from a blow to your self-worth will have filled you with shame. Maybe you have nursed your shame since childhood, eg parents shaming you for not being good enough at something.   Feeling shame is like having a hole in your soul. It can leave you feeling you have failed as a person and are unworthy of love. It isolates you. Your support group will help you learn you are worth while and matter to others.

Let go of any shame. Tell yourself regularly you've always been worth while and good enough. You have an illness like any other illness, and have nothing to be ashamed of. Your no- fault illness made you powerless over alcohol and your behavior unmanageable. Now you trust in your higher power to guide your thoughts, you have stopped your harmful behavior, and changed your personality enough to find recovery.

Negative thoughts keep you from the real business of living. Letting go of them, and worry about people, places and things you can do nothing about, is a choice you can make to rid yourself of anxiety and fear and feel better.

You are powerless over others, but not over your own thoughts. You can change by checking your part in things today and letting go of self will and control.

When you trust in your higher power you will feel a new sense of purpose. Author and Holocaust survivor, Victor Frankyl said 'having a purpose is the corner stone of good mental health'.

Identify your purpose. If you don't know what it is then make a list of what you value and care about and reflect on what matters most to you. If it's all too much for you to think about right now, that's okay. Decide to make sobriety your purpose just for today. Be gentle with yourself while you begin to work at maintaining your recovery. This isn't a rehearsal. This is your real life. So take your time to get better.

If you are happy with your newly changing sober self, life around you will be better, too. Author of 'The power of now' Eckhart Tolle says 'the primary cause of unhappiness is never the situation but your thoughts about it,' meaning happiness really is an inside job

When you are ready to move on, list your strengths and talents. Picture your self being your best possible self and practice being grateful for what you have today.

Ask yourself what difference do you want to make to the world, and what is holding you back from realizing your true purpose in life?

Since the essence of recovery is learning how to feel better about yourself without using alcohol, you are going to have to do something about sorting your flawed thinking and behavior out on a daily basis, eg your resentments, fears and other feelings.

There is no known cure for Aud. You will never be able to drink alcohol safely. But you can manage your illness every day by following a routine to keep you well.

Start by waking up and practicing being grateful and thanking your higher power for another day. Then humble yourself eg getting to the right size by kneeling down and asking your higher power to guide your will for the day. Remember your way never worked. Decide to be happy, because you can choose how you feel, and get on with your day.

Check your self and how you are feeling during the day, asking your higher power for the willingness to let negative feelings go, and replace old behavior with new Talk to another recovering person and go to an Aud meeting. Do something good for someone else unconditionally. Read something new and make a gratitude list when you go to bed. Thank your maker for a sober day and know you are a winner.

Practice your own routine every day for a month and keep going. Life will continue to get better and your new behaviors will become part of your daily life.

Keep your recovery simple, letting your higher power plan your daily work. Don't drink, don't think, get to a meeting in the evening if you can or call someone and share your success, because just for today, you are a winner! How marvelous.

When you have a healthy sleep pattern and three meals a day back in you life and you're feeling happier, healthier and staying sober, think about doing some voluntary work. It will give you a sense of worth and purpose so you start to feel good about yourself and your life. You'll be motivated to get up mornings, look better, feel better, have hope and be empowered to keep moving forward without the pressure of full time employment.

By letting go of your ego you'll have learned a little of the humility necessary for recovery. Your well being and happiness come from inside you, not in acquiring material things or finding new relationships. If you want to feel worth while then you have to discipline yourself to do worth-while things. Use the voluntary opportunity to try something completely new to you. In time it may become something more.

Connecting with nature is proven to be good for your mental health. So take regular walks and get plenty of exercise. Imagine taking a stroll by the sea in a peaceful wild place. Open your own eyes and ears and nose to the sounds and sights and scents around you, birds singing, the smell of the flowers and grass after rain. Think about the variety of wildlife there

All these gifts, given to you by a power greater than yourself, are free to enjoy.

Take time to quietly reflect on your surroundings and things around you. Appreciate the wonderful gifts nature has provided you with. Practice telling the world how grateful you are. Do it until you really are grateful, and glad to be alive. Then everything else will be a bonus, and your life will be rewarding and meaningful again.

What's most fantastic is that you can decide to get grateful whenever you want to. It can begin where ever you are, right away. Get out and get grateful each day and enjoy your life because this isn't a rehearsal, it's the real thing!

Don't let life just happen to you. Make it how you want it to be by choosing what's best for you. Another good reason for giving up alcohol is so you can choose. Notice and appreciate the joy, beauty and happiness in the world. It gets your endorphins going and makes you feel great without the need for alcohol.

As you move forward in your life and learn new ways of living, practice letting go of your old patterns of thinking and behaving, too.

Saying good bye and letting go of a relationship can be difficult if you have forgotten who you were outside of it, eg someone's wife, lover, mother, daughter or friend. But any pain will pass in time. 'Don't smother each other. No one can grow in the shade.'

Dr Love, otherwise known as Professor of Special Education, Leo Buscaglia, American author and motivational speaker said, 'we cannot stop a hurricane, silence a storm, or keep a loved one from leaving us.'

However you can decide to treat your self well and do whatever it takes just for today not to use alcohol. Trust that in time all will be well. Be grateful for the day.

Talking to another recovering person, and sharing how you feel, will help any hurt you have pass quicker. Go to a meeting, or ring someone from your support group and talk it out while you sit down and have a cup of sugary tea.

Doing these few simple things will guarantee your sobriety. Believe me, it works if you work it, and it won't if you don't.

You'll be able to go to Aud support group meetings all over the world, if not in person, on zoom and listen to and learn from hundreds of people who like you suffer from Aud, and have successfully found recovery.

The world is a dynamic and fantastic place full of opportunities. Of course it takes time and practice to develop the habit of letting go of the need to use alcohol. But in time, with discipline and determination, you can let go of your self will and develop a reliable faith in your intuition or higher power to guide you to recovery.

Concentrate on your own well being and taking responsibility for your life.

You can't choose what's right for anyone else. Let them go to live their own life, and learn their own lessons.

Show others by your example, how they can choose to change and grow if they want to. Show them how to find a better way of living for themselves. Whatever happens in others live, it's their business, not yours.

Let go of your care taking behaviors, eg making decisions or taking responsibility for others; sorting the consequences of their choices or piling on advice. Other adults have the right to take care of themselves and come to their own decisions about things. They are not your responsibility.

Building healthy social networks is another important part of recovery.

Talking on a daily basis to others in recovery and getting to a meeting to listen to their experiences is important to helping you learn how to overcome your loneliness in the beginning.

Today you can be exactly how you want to be. That's what quitting alcohol means. And everyday in recovery your life becomes even more joyous and wholly satisfying because I can cope with what ever comes my way. Life happens. It doesn't change, only how I manage it.

What's most fantastic is that you can start changing and feeling better in your life, too, where ever you are, right away, by stopping drinking alcohol eg connect with nature and find a positive reason to get out each day.

Consider different situations that have left you feeling on edge, touchy, and fed up. How did you behave? Did you drink alcohol?

Get serious about letting your higher power guide you, rather than being controlled by your thinking and alcohol. Continue developing faith in your new power.

Faith is easily developed, by taking small steps every day, because faith is simply your belief followed by your action. But you have to make with the action to get the result. Having courage to act on what you believe is creative; because it's your belief that leads to your action that changes you eg thinking creatively of how you will achieve success in your life; designing your daily routine to include time to take care of yourself properly, visualizing something you are making, being finished down to the final details, before it's even started in reality.

Dream big and write down your ideas. Then review them and narrow things down to what really works for you. Because the ASCDE of change shows that who you **Are** is what you **Believe** you **Can Do** about **Everything**.

This may mean deciding to do something different eg learn something new, study, retrain, get some new skills. It's about

Letting go of your resistance to giving up alcohol isn't easy, but it is doable. Those who don't do it, go on to die from their illness. If you grew up with a physical attachment to alcohol, the idea of not being able to turn to a drink for a fix when you want to, probably terrifies you. It's always been there; central to your life. A teaspoonful of alcohol will start off the physical craving for more, again.

It's no good changing drinks, either. Alcohol is alcohol whether it's in mouth wash, mince pies, trifle, marmalade, beer, wine, spirits or chocolates. Have a cup of sugary tea, instead.

Listen to your self the negative words you use, eg won't, can't, shouldn't. Reshape your thoughts and feelings with positive words, like will, can, and could. Let

go of impatience and enjoy every moment of every day you are given.

You know why you're ill and how to change to get recovery. However, determination is essential to your success, allowing you to learn from your mistakes or wrong decisions, without feeling a failure. Failure is part and parcel of your journey to success. If you get knocked back get up and get going again. It's a fact, nothing is ever perfect. But using negative feelings as an excuse to stay stuck is a 'cop out' to doing the work to get well.

German philosopher, Friedrich Nietzsche, once wrote 'He who has a *why* to live for, can bear almost any *'how'*. So, focus on being flexible and resilient when handling problems, by being calm and letting your higher power guide you. You'll learn through your own experience that nothing comes your way in a day that you can't handle with faith in your higher power and your new self to act in a better way.

Mahatma Ghandi was incredibly resilient and adaptable to change, staying in control of situations he faced with Britain inspiring millions by cleverly negotiating complex political landscapes, eg persuading the British Viceroy Lord Irwin to repeal the salt tax.

When you find a cause you really believe in, and take determined action, you can't fail but to get a better outcome eg supporting a newcomer to your Aud group. When you see a persons desperate eyes light up because you have offered them hope and a sure fire way to change, then you will have made a real difference in your life.

To do that, is to give a person their life, again and what a legacy to leave anyone.

Facing the consequences of a chaotic life is never easy. But, you can have hope, because as you work on changing your thinking and feeling you start to change on the inside and everything outside changes, too. Make a daily gratitude list. This is a powerful tool in recovery as a truly grateful alcoholic doesn't want to drink alcohol.

Be grateful, because unlike other fatal illnesses, there is a solution to Aud that allows you to arrest your condition and not die.

Whenever you are knocked back by some problem or new crisis, your desire to find a solution, some meaning or purpose, will act as security to ensure your success. You may not see the benefits of a crisis at first, but if you look for the good in it, and believe it, you will see it. So never give up. Keep going whatever the set back and learn from everything.

As Virginia Satir said 'life is not the way it's supposed to be. It is the way it is. The way you cope with it makes the difference'

If you resolve to see every set back you have as a challenge to teach you something new and strengthen you, self-doubt won't stop you before you start. Focused properly on your goals your resolve can make you a very powerful force. Taking responsibility for all your actions will make you master of your own life so that you can confidently take back control.

The best way to continue to manage your life without needing to use alcohol is to teach someone else. That is why sponsoring others and guiding them to find recovery is such an important part of maintaining your sobriety. It's so incredibly rewarding. To be able to make a positive difference to somebody else suffering Aud is beyond all expectation or anything money can buy, making you the richest person in your world.

Persevere and you will become able to deal with whatever comes your way in a day, without reaching for alcohol. You are responsible for how you feel, so find the courage to do what it takes.

Your future is how you decide to make it. You've worked hard towards recovery and healing from your illness. You've faced your feelings and worked hard on the most harmful problems eg denial, acceptance, forgiveness, powerlessness and unmanageability.

You have learned how to handle and change your feelings and most important of all developed some faith in a higher power so you can let go of control. Now you can choose your actions and live differently, free from the chains of alcohol that bound you to chemical dependence. As you continue to recover from Audkeep yourself in check, sharing what you know with others and practicing gratitude daily. Work hard and enjoy your recovery

Here are a few ideas for non alcoholic flavorsome, fun and healthier soft drinks to treat your self to or enjoy with friends, while giving up alcohol. The recipes are a combination of my own concoctions and some of my health-focused friends. They are simple everyday mixtures of a bit of this and that using as few ingredients as possible.

Giving up alcohol doesn't mean you have to go into hiding under a rock. When you quit drinking alcohol the hardest thing when you go out can be finding a non alcoholic drink you like. But you can look at the challenge of making non alcoholic drinks as a fun thing, and get experimenting at home.

Try using tasty, vitamin-filled fruits, oranges, lemons, pineapple, capsicum, tomato and sparkling water elder flower, mint thyme and soda fizz and crushed ice: whatever you want; herbs, spices fruits and flowers, paprika and honey, lavender, strawberries; the list is endless and many have health benefits, too.

Try making liquorice root tea. It tastes sweet without containing sugar and helps to combat stress and reduce the cravings for alcohol.

Or liquorice and ginger tea

Or anise and lavender tea

Or a combination fruit burst like Strawberry and Melon Juice

Recipe

Combine 75g of chopped strawberries and a slice of water melon with 50g of crushed ice in a food processor and blend until smooth.

Add a tablespoonful of light Agave nectar and blend until smooth.

Peach and Strawberry Juice

Combine one peeled and sliced peach with 75g of chopped strawberries, ¼ cup of peach yogurt and ¼ cup water. Blend until smooth and serve

Raspberry and Orange Juice

Combine a small cup of raspberries with 75g crushed ice and blend.

Add the juice of ½ an orange, 75ml water and a tablespoonful of agave nectar.

Blend and serve.

Try pear and raspberry, apple and raspberry, orange and mango, kiwi and apple, apple and orange juice.

Or a vegetable fix

Recipe

Carrot Juice

Combine ½ cup of water, 125g grated carrot, 1 tsp lemon juice, a pinch of grated root ginger and 25g crushed ice and blend.

Carrot, Coriander and Orange Juice

Combine one grated carrot with the juice of an orange 75ml of water 50g of crushed ice a little lemon juice and blend. Garnish with a sprig of coriander.

Cucumber and Avocado Smoothie

Combine ¼ of a diced cucumber with a ¼ of avocado, a kiwi fruit, ½ cup of semi-skimmed milk 35g plain yogurt, a little lime juice, and 50g crushed ice and blend.

Try beetroot smoothie, spicey tomato juice, red cabbage and apple juice.

Fruit Smoothies

Strawberry Smoothie

Recipe

Combine 125g strawberries with ½ cup semi-skimmed milk, 50g plain yogurt, 25g crushed ice, ¼ lemon 15g caster sugar and blend.

Try banana and pineapple smoothie or pineapple and coconut, or papyra and peach.

www.ingramcontent.com/pod-product-compliance
Lightning Source LLC
Chambersburg PA
CBHW040857120626
46551CB00001B/58